Loranthus

Gauri Jela

INDIA · SINGAPORE · MALAYSIA

For my parents, for passing me some redundant genes that are dominant in neither of them

For my brother, without whom my life would've been very different (in a good way)

For my grandfather and grandmother, for their wholesome goodness

For my daughter, for delaying the completion of this book

For my husband, whose favorite author is me

Author's Note

In school, I was that girl who was noticed by my Maths teachers and English teachers alike. I was terribly bad at Maths and terrific at language papers, and I used to amuse myself thinking of a staffroom conversation between the two of them. My then headmaster, Sir Alex Fernandez, was the one who truly made an effort to express the belief he had in my writing skills. He called my parents and informed them that I was to study English Literature. He had read a story of mine in the school magazine and was genuinely moved. I can safely say that he is my first 'reader' and also the first one to believe in me.

After I went on to become a Civil Engineer and realized that I was going to be a mediocre engineer at best, I believed in my headmaster and myself. I went on to be an English teacher, a content writer, and then a technical writer at corporate companies. After my daughter was born, I had a break from work and decided to write whenever I could. It did not happen as regularly as I wanted to, but it definitely was a starting point.

These poems are mostly from the times I stared into nothingness, was not thinking of anything specific, and then suddenly a thought finding its way to me. Some of them are from my childhood memories; some are purely born out of imagination. There are also poems written by a sperm, a bottle of wine, and a parasitic plant – like Loranthus.

In the home I grew up, there was this humongous mango tree that adorned our front yard. It bore delicious mangoes—one of the very first memories of my perception of taste. Writing about it, my mouth waters like I already have a bowl of that diced golden delight—sweeter as it has the scent of my childhood. Loranthus sometimes claimed parts of her and, in the end, consumed the whole of her. This book of poetry is an ode to everything that was conducive to weaving me into what I am. Loranthus is a part of my childhood—one of the first few memories of hurt, of letting go and of waiting for the next season.

I have always thought about the mystery of a piece of fiction. It starts from a single thought and becomes this whole big jungle (or garden, however you want to look at it). Once the piece is written, the writer turns a reader, in fact, the first reader. So who is the actual writer? Whatever the force that resides in a writer or a painter (or anybody who creates 'magic from thin air') is, I want to thank 'it' for letting them be the medium. So, dear force, thank you for letting me be the medium.

And you. Thank you for picking this book.

Foreword by the Author

For an amateur writer like me, who hid away everything I wrote, to come out in the light and collect these pieces in one place, is much like being vulnerable and raw in a new space. I would like to thank all those who have helped me in different phases of this journey of being out here.

Sabi Salim, my best friend and writer, who always tells me that I write well.

Sir Alex Fernandez, former headmaster of Christ Nagar Senior Secondary School, for giving that call to my home and talking to my parents because he loved a story I wrote for the school magazine in 2009.

Rev. Fr. Dr. Mathew Thengumpally CMI, former Principal of Christ Nagar Senior Secondary School, for giving me opportunities to explore my love for writing through countless literary competitions.

My grandfather, for always patiently reading my poems and stories and for being my biggest pillar.

Tillu, my close friend and confidant, for never filtering feedback and opinions on my works.

My father, for taking time to read what I wrote and making me feel heard.

My mother, for being my biggest critic and cheerleader.

My husband, for reminding me to keep writing.

Prajwal Subramanian, for suggesting to me the biggest writing platform I've ever been on.

Maji, for spending countless hours working on the face of my dream—the cover page.

A few of my close friends who told me I should get published.

Kunju, my greatest gift, for being a patient, loving mother to me when she feels one isn't enough for me.

Contents

Contents

1   Red Wine

A bottle of thin blood,
Perched in the front row,
On a rustic shelf,
In a home that glows.

I watch birthdays, sweet reunions,
Promotions, partings—joy and tears,
Laughter rising, voices softening,
As I count the passing years.

My name is whispered, hushed and low,
My age discussed in fleeting breath,
Like a secret princess in her tower,
Veiled in silence, bound by depth.

I yearn to spill, to touch warm lips,
To linger there, embraced, adored,
To set alight the senses deep,
Yet, in my glass, I stay ignored.

Contained, untouched—a virgin still,
Oblivious to the heat of men,
Uncertain of the tease and thrill,
Will I ever taste their sin?

I could be wings to those who sip,
A muse to thoughts that dare to stray,
Yet hope within me flickers thin,
As dawn arrives, day fades.

The morning calls for tea,
And I am left untouched, alone.
I breathe myself—my aging scent,
Stronger now than I have known.

2   Taste that Lingers

If I were your favorite meal,
I'd want to be all you see,
The taste you crave, the thought you chase,
The dream you wanna wake up to.

No matter how the spices call,
Or tempting dishes gleam,
Through every scent and whispered name,
I'd be your only choice.

I want to hear you say my name,
"I love it—nothing more.
I wouldn't share a single bite,
I want it, mine alone."

I want to see impatience spark,
As I take my time to arrive,
Hear you ask with fidgeting hands,
"Is it ready? I'm hungry."

To taste, to touch, to claim my heat,
To lift me, hold me tight,
Like something rare, a long-lost feast,
Now found within your sight.

Click your pictures, whisper *wow*,
Let hunger light your face,
Let your lips anticipate,
The warmth of my embrace.

Part me gently, let me breathe,
Let my steam rise soft and high,
Take your cutlery and taste—
Let me melt, let flavors sigh.

I want to see your lashes fall,
To hear you hum, eyes closed,
To feel your heat, to make you sweat,
To set your pulse exposed.

Let me in—consume me whole,
Let my fire burn you through,
Savor me until you say,
"I'd choose this taste anew."

I'll linger in your deepest core,
A hunger you can't quell,
A craving that returns in waves,
A longing you know well.

Let me be your heat, your rush,
Your pulse, your heart, your breath,
Until we merge—one taste, one touch,
Together, even in death.

3 Forsaken and Forgotten

One among millions-
In hibernation for long,
Until I was given life-
Though for a brief while.

Not a life for myself,
But the giver of it-
Meaningless by myself-
Wondrous in creation.

Never grew up,
But I watched
A thousand deaths-
Those who never made it.

Wish I had a mouth,
A nose and little arms
To eat and sniff,
To hold and let go.

People died all the time,
No eulogies for funerals.
Copious amounts of bodies,
Too tiny for the big world.

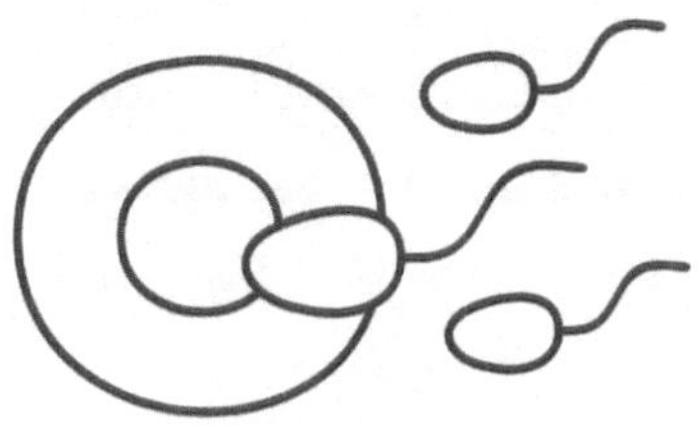

It was many years back
That we mourned the first massacre,
Little did we know
That death was our 'way to life'.

Those banished
Remained mum about the slumber.
Their cries drowned
In loud moans of pleasure.

When my day came,
I was jolted awake.
Pushed out among others,
Like water out of a broken pipe.

The few of us who saw the light-
Were gone forever.
A few others moved forward
Another darkness, another home.

'The fastest and strongest-
Will be chosen to live in daylight'.
Said the headless old man.
For us, daylight meant death.

Life awaits, where daylight
Would no longer be dreadful.
I rushed forward for home-
It was not just darkness in there.

There were a couple of girls
Round and cute,
Ready to embrace us.
I seared one of them slightly.

My head smashed at her wall-
I closed my eyes for the last time-
Watching her dance with another lad-
There ended my silly life.

Unknown, unspoken of,
Unnamed and unseen,
My death is not mourned,
For I was only the second best.

4 Bloodline

She swiped some bright red
On to her luscious lips.
Like fresh blossoms,
Like they deserved a slight touch.

Her heels clacked as she walked,
Great depths in her eyes.
Her nose just the right size,
The diamond pin like a far away star.

She was the night sky,
My eyes made constellations in her.
Her fingers so slender and long,
Clipped nails in red that matched her lips.

She walked past me,
Into the room that read-
"Chief of Neurosurgery".
Her grace belonged everywhere.

Her fingers and eyes-
Seeing and feeling things
Not for faint-hearts like me,
Stories of various brains!

Some complex than the others-
The fragility of life.
She was the night sky,
She owned the constellations.

She drew and redrew them,
For those whose heads she landed on,
Literally and otherwise.

When she called my name,
Little did I know that
She was gonna open mine,
And red would be my last memory.

5 Fate in Blush Pink

The street, a furnace of heat and haste,
Men and women rushing.
Scorching sun, a blade on my skin,
Draining the breath from deep within.

Palming my cheek, fingers damp,
Sweat tracing paths through the heat,
Shadows stretch, twist, and slide,
My own glides, silent, by my side.

Then one stops.
Stiff, still, near mine,
A pause in motion, a fractured line.
My breath halts, a pulse gone astray.

As his shadow lingers, refusing to sway.
I seek his face, already there,
Eyes like embers, knowing, aware.
A smile, sly, barely formed.

His gaze flickers to the wall, then me,
A step forward, the earth feels free.
The air thickens, the scent of dust and sweat,
A moment drawn in fate's fine net.

From the corner of my lips, he lifts,
A ring—blush pink, delicate, adrift.
Soft as rose petals, warm as breath,
A whisper grazes the space between:

"I know you, don't I?"

The words, a thread through time's unseen seam.
And when he kissed me, the world stood still-
Our shadows, too, beneath the spill
Of golden dusk and fleeting light.

6 The Last Day of Childhood

On days I whined
And refused to shower
My father bathed me.

Luxurious lather
Smeared on me,
A snowman was made.

Bubbles blown to him,
As he rubbed off ink marks-
"Why do you draw on your skin?"

As I royally ignored him
And made bigger bubbles,
He popped 'em all!

The day I grew up,
I wrapped myself
In my small bath towel.

Stepped into my dad's room,
To check my closet
For a dress to change to.

He stopped at the door-
Draped in a skimpy towel,
Was my eleven-year old self.

Weeks away from first period,
Oblivious to the changes
In my body that housed a kid.

"Change in the bathroom",
His voice was deep,
Stern and clear.

"But on the wet floor,
I would trip and fall-
Get hurt."

"Lock the room,
And then change."
His stubbornness was solid.

No more lather soaked me in.
My childhood snapped
Like those bubbles I made.

The last days of my childhood-
Balancing myself on wet floor,
And taking care not to trip over.

The night my father told his girl,
"You have grown up",
My body ceased to house the kid.

7   The Cheiro Palmist

When your palm is on mine
I hold the whole world.
Let me read yours,
I'd love to try.

The faint spirals
On your fingertips,
Aren't they similar
To the ones on mine?

When I decrypt yours,
Would they yell my name-
And mine, yours?
Destined to be, are we?

My fingertips
Over those gazillion lines
That cross your palms,
Do some of them bleed?

If only I could be a line in your palm-
Not be there at your first cry,
Appear when the time is right.
Age with you, grow deeper.

Out on your palm,
Is the real you, innit?
Nobody knows you entirely,
But those faint lines.

Am I not already one of them?
I know your broken lines
And the solid ones-
You gave yourself away to me.

8   Saree

Wrapping myself in my mother's dupatta,
I put on my dad's spectacles.

I looked like my favorite teacher.
I asked my little brother,
To do his homework-
Before he came to my class.

Neatly plated cotton saree
That my professor draped.

My grandmother's saw weddings,
Funerals and ground coconut,
Crushed the pallu in her fist,
Half-dead pleats flat on her chest.

My favorite artists had theirs
No longer than the dupatta.

Mother's saree was always green,
With mustard yellow border,
Much like the turmeric and curry leaves,
She always smelled of.

Mother draped a saree for me.
I felt a little like her.

A hundred pins to hold it,
I walked like a duck
Not meant to wear one
Or look graceful as much.

Parts of me uncovered,
Touched by fresh air.

As years became decades,
My grandmother's sarees
Adorned my wardrobe
Shades of all colors.

I became a little like her,
And a little like my mom.

For though I wore grandma's sarees,
I wore them the way mom did.

The Poet

Tall and proud are the beings
Whose gestation is indefinite.

Pregnancy that outlives
Menopause and wrinkled skin.

Lonely eggs left loners,
Until the bearer hatches them.

Millions of words and thoughts,
Dying, not knowing birth.

Oh, dear poet! Do you not know?
The magic that you easily carry around.

I beseech you, don't kill them.
Birth them—over a coffee or tea.

Birth them—the loners.
If you'd let them

They are timeless.
Outliving you—the sorcerer.

Look at them with compassion,
Watch your baby thoughts grow.

Branch them out or tie them up,
But set them free as you breathe life.

Words that travel far and wide,
Away from you and places you know.

But always tethered to you,
Like the moon is to our world.

They'll remember your name,
Long after you forget the same.

Some of your life left behind,
A part of you left behind,

About perceptions and misconceptions,
Denying you a complete death.

Embalmed and preserved,
Worshiped and quoted.

Poets live two lives,
More honored in the second.

10 Lullaby

I was a couple of feet tall,
Threw my arms around my mom,
Held her by her thighs, and
Listened to her raging belly.

Eyes widened at the voices inside-
Churning and grinding,
A pretty loud affair
That only I heard.

On nights I cried in my sleep,
I lay on her, ear against her tummy-
Listening to the chaos-
A lullaby to me, until dawn.

When my mom started eating for two-
My hungry little brother growing in her,
I touched her big round belly
And listened to my brother gurgling.

The eve of my exam-
Sleep, a distant dream.
My head on my granny's torso,
Twisting and turning until I listened again.

Tummies make the best music
I was convinced,
Tuning in to it to zone out.
Soon, I had a baby growing in mine.

Ears after ears pressed against me,
Talking sweet little words
And caressing the fully round bump,
Stretch marks that drew rainbows.

Last night, my little one cried so loud,
She could not be soothed, and
I put her on me- she hugged me tight,
She listened to my stomach until asleep.

Today she told me-
"Mamma, I was inside you,
Your belly, yesterday."
She smiled wide.

It took me three decades
And a baby—my third eye,
To realize why my favorite lullaby
Was the voice inside the tummy.

11 Black

On black days,
I'm a turtle.
Limbs and head in my shell,
Hiding in the Mariana Trench.

Days I wish to disappear,
Be gone, be forgotten.
I know I'm lost-
Don't wanna be found.

My mind yells 'enough'.
Not loud enough for me,
Or shake me up.
I'm angry, shouting louder.

I'm nothing; I'm a blip.
I don't live on black days.
Black days glare at me
On other black days.

I scream until I'm blue,
The days I stare at my phone,
The days I curl in my bed,
And not let my mom near me.

Those days laugh at me,
And I dig a hole to bury myself.
I refuse to cry out loud,
For you don't know my battles.

The numerous deaths and shame,
Torn boots on my feet to walk nail beds,
Pulling out knives and needles-
Red, gushing out like a broken tap.

I survive black days,
I wear black on white days,
Because black also offered quick death,
Yet, here I am.

12 The Little Girl

"Cherub, I wanna meet God."
"Little girl, why, may I know?"
"I need to talk to him…"
"You have all the time…"

On the first day in heaven,
The little girl ran down the rainbow.
Her great granddaddy said,
"You're too early, kiddo."

The little girl smiled,
And ran away saying
She wanted Cherub
Help her meet God.

On the seventh day,
She was watching a newborn coo,
And laugh, when
Cherub walked up to her.

"God wants to meet you…"
Her smile faded,
She walked the road to God.
Cherub guided her.

God wore white,
And had gentle eyes.
"I have a request,"
Said the little girl.

"My last life, I loved candies.
A man gave me candies
To do things to my body
He touched me places-

Places that are secret.
I was hardly three,
Right and wrong
Were gray zones.

A twisted idea of love
In my little mind,
Candies crushed in my hand
As I clenched it in pain.

God, I was six
When he smothered me,
Because I cried a little
Out of gut-wrenching pain.

Heat of my tears
Burned my eyes and cheeks,
Fire of his dark desire,
Turned me into ashes.

I left my body,
When pain blinded me.
Like a flower,
I lay in his grip—crushed.

The stillness of death,
Nor my incomplete cries,
Brought fear or worry,
He smiled at my body.

Clicked his tongue,
"What a shame!"
He forced open my fist
My little fingers broke.

He picked a melted candy,
Popped it in mouth,
As he tied a rope,
Around my neck.

As I hung from the ceiling,
He spat the candy,
The final homage,
Drenched in my sweat and his spit.

It was a short life, I'm told,
But it felt like a long one.
Sticky hands that smelled of sugar,
And muffled cries drenched in tears.

God, if I'm to be born again,
Please, let me live a little more.
To make friends,
To make promises.

To feel the water against my skin,
Wind in my hair,
To make little bouquets,
And send them out with a grin.

To write and speak big words,
For my mom to doll me up,
To know her and my dad,
And to give them back, doubled.

Please, Lord, next time,
Make me hate candies,
Or make me sickly and weak,
I can't wait to live a full life—or death.

13 Happy Abuse

A double line,
A little me inside,
Stronger by the day.

Balloon for a belly,
Lemons turning melons,
Hair growing luscious.

A spider web of veins on chest,
Wild thoughts in mind,
Hormones crawling all over.

A dark line down the tummy,
Once poised belly button,
Now contorted and unalluring.

Legs broken at the knees,
Bent spinal cord,
Heads of the melon drooping.

Bracing up to fuel life,
Like a juggler—three balls on my torso,
And the tinier fourth button.

All excited with weight gain,
Crushed spine and knees,
Mind racing as I die.

Heart ready to give out while birthing,
Housing life was a breeze,
Showing the world a hurricane.

Weak life suckling,
On my sore melons,
Pumping milk, blood, or both.

Tender breasts chewed on,
Sharpness knew no mercy.
The droop—the withering flowers.

Bump stretched out,
Turning mature white,
After being young blue and teenage violet.
The happy body abuse that this is.

14 The Diamond Nosepin

It took all my savings,
To buy that solitaire pin,
Which always adorned,
My big, flat nose.

The chocolate skin,
Complimented my shiny pin,
The flatness of my nose forgotten,
At the gleaming new addition.

The night of my wedding,
I was told that the solitaire,
Had a sheen that looked so much
As the shine in my eyes.

Hardly ten days passed
Before I was slapped hard,
"He has a bad temper,"
Chuckled his mother.

My nose turned red,
And the solitaire sat,
In a tiny pool of red,
Refusing to drip down.

The sindoor on my hairline,
The bangles in my hands,
A dot of ruby around the pin,
Red was what I saw on me.

It took me two years
To walk out of the red.
Home was far away,
Solitaire bridged the distance.

Happy to give away,
What I proudly wore.
Happy that it could take me home,
Back to the safe space.

Back in my home,
I was freed from red,
Chuckles were not evil,
And I was the solitaire.

On my thirtieth birthday,
My father gifted me,
Yet another nosepin-
A gush of memories.

"Flaunt your nose,
And your growth,"
It had a sheen that looked so much
As the shine in my eyes.

15 Raw

Always craved stories,
Grandpa told me
About civilizations and wars,
Renaissance and revolution.

I read and reread history,
Stories that I could now narrate,
Dates and timelines in my mind,
Chronology and names firm.

History books had white facts,
With specks of gray.
Blindfolded eyes of mine,
And I believed that I knew it all.

Atrocities of Columbus,
Brown Britishers in colonization,
Biased stories, narrow perspectives,
Twisted stories, unseen past.

Truths were loud grays,
I adored the wrong people,
Grays jolted me awake,
My textbook was a lie.

Would accounts of the past
All over the world
Say the same stories?
Are all names painted white?

Could I read the past again,
This time with no adulteration,
So that brutality of truth,
May not shock me anymore.

Cruelty, betrayal, torture and the unfair,
I will know why the world as it is,
Is only a projection
Of an unknown past.

Can I know about the world today,
Through unadulterated stories?
May I burn this veil of disguise,
And bare the parts that need light?

16   Harmless Lies

When my cousin told me
About the intricate painting
She had made as if
She were a prodigy,

I was naive and awed,
The painting was beautiful,
And I asked her about
The making of its elements.

She talked with passion,
Sparkle in her eyes,
Pride in her talent,
Humble to share her learnings.

When she told me it was a lie,
I was lost.
Her effortless lies
Had my full attention.

Comprehending that 'lie'
Took longer than I thought.
"I was just joking"
She said and laughed at me.

"Harmless lie," she said.
Deception in her eyes,
Pride in her talent,
Hunger to watch my trust shatter.

Among liars who hatch lies
To hold together their happy world,
And those who lie
For the joy they find in breaking faith,

I'm scared of the latter.
For they could be smiling
While my trust fools me,
And lets them laugh hard.

17 Backward Train

My childhood is a bright white,
A plain paper that took in
The weight of all the words,
Yellow with time, but fresh.

My childhood is in the front yard,
Where I rode the tricycle,
Tasted the flowers and smelled the sand,
Bruised my knees and cried after.

Teenage took that cozy chair in verandah,
Under the warm yellow light,
That subtly heated up the air,
Just enough to let me cook my poems.

My teenage is warm yellow
And smells of my grandma's Gita.
It sounds like my grandpa's heavy breaths,
And his big-belly laugh.

Unannounced battles in my mind,
Looks that seemed to matter much,
Braced teeth and flat hair,
Dented self-esteem and the quiet.

As an adult, I lived in my room.
The front yard and the verandah,

Awaited me all the while,
I became my room—its scent mine.

I took birth in the front yard,
And it would see me next
Only when I am sixty,
If I ever decided to water those sprouts.

At thirty, everything changed
But one thing,
This moment here,
And the bliss I feel.

The same I enjoyed
As an innocent child,
A troubled teenager,
A mature adult.

Cook some poems,
Mine some stories,
While I break a sweat,
And pause to revisit.

18 Chambers in my Head

"Are you lost?"
I'm asked often.
"Your mind is elsewhere,"
I'm told often.

I'm a prisoner
Of my own thoughts,
Locked in four walls,
No space to breathe.

The ringing in the Venus,
Triggers and trauma,
Overthinking the hmm's
Sent by a friend a decade back.

They come to me in waves,
Gushing and foaming,
Loud and salty,
Breaking and building me.

I sit and simmer
In the awe and bliss
Of my own thoughts,
As the present pulls me out.

People take away
My awe and sanity,
Gatecrashing my peace,
Asking me where I'm lost.

If my head had chambers,
To hold my thoughts,
I'd spend half my life,
Sorting the keys to the right ones.

I'd hide away a few,
And forget about what they hold,
I'd have a few favorites,
That I would unlock in the evenings.

I'd open them in the still,
Close them away otherwise,
So that I live both worlds,
Neatly tucking each other away.

19 Love in Summer

On summer evenings
When the air is all dry,
And our lips chapped,
I want you.

Sweat tickling our back,
While we yearn,
For water or each other,
The heat would dissolve lines.

We would get sunburns,
And we would strip naked
To escape the sheer swelter
That pricks us through our clothes.

When I turn so red,
The littlest of your words
Would irk me much,
My mind would be set ablaze.

Our temper testing our love
And our love testing our temper.
Love trying to find a shade
In the dying embers of hope.

Seeking water to drench ourselves,
While our sweat wrinkles our skin
Love in its long slumber,
Hoping to wake up to a cool breeze.

Water will wake love up,
The first few layers of dry air
And parched skin will need water.
Would we last summer evenings?

Would we still hold hands
And feel each other's sweaty palms?
If we do, I want you
To kiss my red skin blue.

20 Cobwebs of Childhood

Dolled up in a red dress,
I touched up my maroon lips.
"Can't do tonight, babe,"
He said, crashing in the bed.

Tired, he was,
Yelled his sweaty shirt and soiled shoes,
A seed of betrayal
Found its way to my heart.

Betrayal sprouted,
A tiny sapling,
Leaves growing giant,
Roots going deeper.

I felt as tall as the tree,
And saw an axe of a person
In my exhausted husband,
Who couldn't take me out.

Trust went for a vacation,
Fear came to stay.
Overthinking tagged along,
Sorrow pulled a chair.

I felt myself trembling,
As a bunch of uninvited guests
Paraded in and messed me up,
Sending an army of tears.

My husband disappeared,
He was an axe entirely,
Aiming at the tall tree that I was,
Threatening my existence.

I was an overreacting wife,
Disrespecting his need to rest,
Denying him the time to recharge,
Unwilling to cancel plans.

A long night,
An open conversation,
And a coffee later,
My eyes had their sight back.

I was not a tree,
He was not an axe.
That evening was familiar-
My childhood, draped in a red dress.

Years of denial,
Lost hope and joy,
'Next time' that never came,
'Not today' that I heard often.

A long time of being scared,
To be happy and excited,
At a simple dinner plan,
Or a Sunday picnic.

Broken promises, hollow words,
Being unheard and denied,
Sending in people after people,
That sat on my branches.

Mindful words, tacit nods,
Warm hugs and unflinching love,
Were the way to my tranquility,
And the only way to me.

Years into adulthood,
Yet it only took a little blow,
To make me that hopeless child,
Who had forgotten to smile.

21 The Bee

Oh! You drink me up!
You leave me so empty!

Your tiny legs kiss away
A bunch of my pollen.

And your lips are dripping
Of the sweet nectar that's mine.

But go, dear friend,
Tell someone I'd never meet

About the folds of my petals,
And the flavor of my honey.

Come back to me,
With the essence of him,

Leave inside me,
A part of him and his scent.

I'll blush pink when I see
Tiny little blooms at my tips.

I'll wait for you to tell me,
If they look like me or him.

You should tell them
About the man their dad is.

And one day, when I wither away,
Take my petal and lay it inside him.

I shall sleep in his arms,
And wake up to his warmth.

22 Comfort

At therapy, walked in a girl.
She wanted a name
For her diary.
I told her, "Name it after you!"

Ink blots on some pages,
Never thought of affirmations
Or kind words for herself,
Always sought them elsewhere.

Wrote much about
Her small, sunken eyes.
Never about the world
She saw through those little windows.

Ranted about the big nose,
Slyly talked about it,
For validation and acceptance,
Never about that nose pin she wanted.

Rabbit teeth
In the confines of braces
That pushed them back much
Not once, but twice.

Gummy smiles and braces-
The graveyards of her self-esteem,
Nervous, careful laughter,
That hid it all behind her fingers.

Walked away from mirrors,
Ran to darkness,
Walked away from parties,
Ran to isolation.

Tamed her demons,
While offers were made
To 'fix' her hair,
And 'fix' her wardrobe.

Pushed and kicked
Her way out to herself,
Redid her hair,
And reorganized her closet.

She met herself outside,
She looked disheveled,
Happiest when left alone,
Troubled in company.

Today, she has learned to trust,
To sing out loud,
Embrace herself,
Without make up.

While things go wrong,
She forgives her.
When people come to 'fix' her,
She sends them back.

Comfort.
If not she herself, nobody else.

23 The Artist's Lover

"Artistic and smart,"
Said the world about her.
A thousand colors
In her canvas.

A gazillion strokes,
Symbolisms and references,
In the revolutionary masterpiece
That she birthed overnight.

"A class apart,"
Wrote columnists.
"How brilliantly beautiful,"
Whispered her contemporaries.

I've been there, on her way-
To heights I still can't see.
Nights she ignored me,
Hurt she caused me, and herself.

She was a silly thought,
A short-lived lie,
Broken shard of glass,
That hid under my skin.

Way to her greatness,
Was a narrow path for me.
Of unflinching love,
Relentless commitment.

Of being the stubborn fingers
That played the guitar,
Through building callus,
And waiting for the painless day.

I disappear into darkness,
In her blindingly bright light,
Pride beaming in my eyes,
As her light blinds me.

24 The Recluse

Friendship barges in
Discord,
In my otherwise aloof self.

Shaking me awake
Violent,
While I was inside my shell.

Threats to break it
Disorientation,
In and around.

I was never ready, but
Stubborn,
That they be let in.

"That, in your eyes
Turquoise,
Is that a crayon?"

"How's your day going?"
Halted,
On my way to a busy morning.

They caught me
Off-guard,
I was in my little space.

Time worked for us
Closer,
Investing in each other.

A quick tea or a walk
Deliberate,
Were the efforts to bond.

A few of them, though-
Shadows
Of their former selves.

People flow on their own-
Currents,
Turbulent and strong.

A home was found
Away,
Away from my shell.

I found home here
Company,
That gave me warmth and hope.

Coffees and sandwiches
Vulnerable,
Enough to rely on them.

And then our lines fall out
Imbalance,
Diminishing efforts and pain.

Just one more evening
Disentangle,
The little knots, shall we?

All those strains
Serenity,
And unconditional love.

Shall we press them out?
Happier,
Let us be, one last time.

25 Ocean's Whiff

She disarmed me,
Threw away my facades.

Like amoeba is to human,
I stood there before her.

She rumbled loud,
My despair sang with hers.

Washing away my sins,
She kissed my feet.

Also buried me bit by bit,
My feet deep in her pit.

The sky, with his vastness,
Pretended to have her.

She was growing younger,
Her advancing shoreline shouted.

All the more playful,
Chasing after sprightly kids.

Her roar as fierce as ever,
Aiming at me for a hug.

Loving the world at her abode,
Undividedly, thoroughly.

Picnics, dates, birthdays,
Kisses, walks, conversations,

Backdrop of all memories,
Constant, humbling, intriguing.

She rumbles at me,
Invites me in.

"Closer, closer," she murmurs,
"Come back here," warns life.

Baby crabs like little spiders,
Collectors of unspoken words.

Seashells like hungry lovers,
Waltzing in with young sands.

My secrets sleep in her bed,
The ones she washed away.

Resurrecting most of them—
I'm salty when I'm home.

26 Old Kisses

Your kisses are home,
From an old time.
Five decades of life,
And I thought I'm done.

My grandma rushing,
To soothe my swollen arms.
Wetting where my mom's
Stick kissed my tender skin.

Heap of chocolates
Mom placed on my table.
Favorite dishes,
Even when I forget about them.

Grandpa's love,
Was as big as his plate.
"Careful," he said,
As I munched on that crab.

Serious love was my dad's,
Devoid of words
Or loud professing,
Godlike presence, guarded.

Then marched in lovers,
To break love, build trust.
Break trust and hit restart-
Brick by brick, a piece at a time.

Love could be sleeplessness,
Hawk eyes of friends,
Half cooked lies,
Burned pizzas and cold breeze.

Love could also be lustful,
Or plain platonic,
Excitement, disappointment,
Desperation and exhilaration.

When my kind of love came,
I was fifty-one—a wife, a mother.
Love needn't be rebuilt,
Restart was only the beginning.

I was eighteen, in love,
He was twenty-six,
With another girl,
Measuring love in cups.

I was twenty-eight,
Mom of two,
He had three-
Busy parents to our own.

At fifty-one,
Sensible and solemn,
I meet a witty fifty-nine,
One that made sixty blush.

We talked on day one,
And we were on day ninety,
We only paused-
To eat, bathe and sleep.

Time only matters
To the body that we house.
Isn't the soul that houses this body,
Timeless?

Because sometimes,
Love is complete,
When you know
He is out there.

Your love for me,
I want them to be
My mom's kisses.
Old, but familiar. Home.

27 The Underrated Pleasure

I walked in,
The hollow chair
Called out to me.

Fear enveloped me
As I sat there,
Hoping for time to fly.

But time chose to freeze,
Sweat broke out,
As I almost cried.

"You don't belong here,"
I told the gurgle in my tummy,
"Leave me for once. Please."

I walked out,
After what felt like eternity.
"Did it pass?"

Asked my loving mom.
I shook my head
And heaved a sigh.

Mom wiped a tear,
"Have a banana,"
She offered.

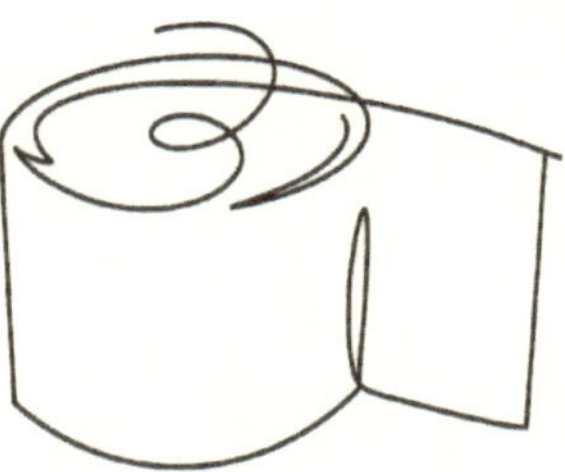

Food was a nightmare,
I wished I could be pregnant,
With all that I ate.

I wished my body held on
For a couple of months.
I wanted to eat in peace.

Hunger has a way
Of blinding my mind
And sneaking food into me.

Such was that moment,
When the banana sneaked in,
Restarting my gurgling stomach.

I ran, fearing I'd soil the hall,
On the hollow chair I sat,
Awaiting a painless pass.

The faucet in my hand,
I awaited the push,
Much like a lady in labor.

At the slightest hint,
I sprayed myself warmth,
A midwife's tale I hoped to work.

Slight thumping at my rear,
As I refuse to push,
I'm already torn, the pain weakens me.

"Please God, please,"
I whisper to myself,
Faucet still cheering me on.

Reminiscing the good old times,
When it took tens of seconds
To be done with my business.

Trying hard to be calm,
As I struggle to tame my mind,
I squeeze my eyes close.

I curl forward,
My chest touching my knees,
I exert myself with all my might.

"Plop!" It was to me,
What a baby's cry is to a new mom.
My eyes welled up.

I kept spraying myself,
The happy rain,
That my rear much deserved.

28 Loranthus

I'm a clingy lover,
Of the woods
You lovingly tend to.

I'm no heartbreaker,
Yet when love sprouts
I seldom stop.

Flowering mango trees,
Sowing a hundred yellow mangoes
In your mind, day and night.

Little would you know
That your tree is taken
For my love hugs so tight.

Her hairs turning red,
My buds her tiara,
Us, entwined.

Her food turns mine,
Her flowers forget to bloom,
Under the sun and the moon.

You spot me and scream at me,
Hugging her tighter, I yell at you-
"Stop taking away her fruits.

She loves them on her,
Her little children,
She wants to watch them grow.

You pluck them early,
Pickle them and savor them,
Provide them warmth and shade,

While they're meant to thrive
Out here, with her.
She wants to live with me.

The rest of her life,
Childless, in peace, love and hugs.
Stop eyeing her!"

We know your callousness,
And our impending fate,
We hug each other tighter.

Until one day,
You cut her hair
That holds me.

I fall down,
A strong thud as I hit the ground.
A piece of her down with me.

I look up to her,
Her tears drop on me.
I smile through my own.

Holding on
To the little piece of her,
I walk away from my love.

A little of me still unseen,
On another part of her,
Ready to embrace her.

I'm no heartbreaker,
Yet when love sprouts,
I seldom stop.

29 The Handwriting

Like rustling dry leaves,
The old paper cried,
Because his pen never stopped,
Not even when the paper tore.

His handwriting slanting,
Much to the left,
An orchestrated dance,
Between the letters.

I read his poem,
Beautiful, like a garden,
Blooming, little flowers,
Flying around, little ladybugs.

My eyes watered them,
Ink smeared from the corner.
Words disappeared,
Pain stayed.

The void filled me up,
Much to my brim,
"Let us out"- loud chatter,
I sit down to write.

Pen sits snug,
But doesn't belong there.
Have I forgotten my letters?
Won't they dance, too?

As I hold my phone,
Typing away my thoughts,
My fingertip heats up,
Words shot from them—bullets.

Self-inflicted wounds,
Phone screen mirroring hurt,
Onward and upward,
A body of holes in the end.

30 Out of Love

When we fell out of love,
Was I scrubbing the plates?
Were you watching the news?

When love wanted to leave,
Did we know?
Had we seen it coming?

When the door creaked,
Had we paused to notice?
Did we listen to who it was?

When we stopped caring,
Was I on your lap, sleeping?
Did you lean in for one last kiss?

How long did we wait?
For the other to realize,
And to bring it up?

Was it our child who told us?
Was it your mom?
It's certainly not either of us.

When I packed my bags
To that business trip,
Why did you hand me the keys?

When you pressed your shirts,
Was it because you knew?
That you'll be by yourself?

How long before we finally talk?
About the bed growing bigger?
And the dreams emptier?

31 The Housewife

The finger cuts from mornings-
Reality checks that wake me up
From the blissful nothingness
My mind wanders away to.

Like a mechanical chopper,
I frantically cut vegetables,
To mix with pulses,
Or even more vegetables.

My mind, numb with the options,
My brain paralyzed,
Watching the time
And the number of whistles.

Factoring in delays and worst cases,
Anxious about leftovers going stale,
Eyes on the clock every now and then,
More tired by the second.

Looking for things that are always in blind spots,
The knife that I just used,
Or the salt or the chili flakes,
Like they're always taken away.

It never feels lonely in there,
With a toddler of an absent mind,
Messing around itself,
Running in circles inside circles.

Along with the dishes,
I serve a little bit of myself too,
A few drops of my blood,
And a sheath of my skin.

Sometimes I cook myself
In the heat of the kitchen,
And then, when I'm sweaty,
It feels like I'm closed with a lid.

To grow smooth like caramelized tomatoes,
Or like the overcooked beef on the stove,
Or the watery curries that flow everywhere,
Simmering until they're dry and ready.

Just like the things in the kitchen,
Have I turned a blind spot too?
There, but not quite,
Near, but far to reach.

32 As a Mom

On an evening,
A decade or so later,
You might find an old picture,
Of you and I.

You'll probably laugh
At my hair color and make up,
You'd find it unbelievable,
That I used to be young once.

I'll laugh with you,
And find it unbelievable myself-
For my youth was all yours,
I was busy making it all memorable.

I would tell you,
How we used to cuddle together,
About your food choices,
And best friends back then.

You'd probably not remember
Most of them.
You'll perhaps learn new things about yourself,
As I walk you through the old days.

I'll tell you how I was exhausted
Because you wouldn't sleep.
How it tired me out,
That my energy couldn't match up yours.

I'll also tell you
How, as a two-year-old,
You gave me the tightest hugs,
And loveliest kisses.

How, as a four-year-old,
You offered me the last piece of chocolate,
And always told me that you love me,
When you sensed I was sad.

How we had each other,
How we stood up for each other,
How we learned and explored together,
The world that we saw together.

I'd tell you that I feel so old,
And you'll laugh at that and say,
"Because you are old,"
I'd ache a little for not having grown younger.

If age could go in reverse,
I'd still be chasing you down,
Tickling you and cuddling with you,
We'd have done that forever and ever.

We'll walk this road often,
For I've planted memory triggers
Everywhere for you to find them,
So that I walk this beautiful road yet again.

33 Sabi

When she was happy,
It was first in her eyes.
Once it touched her lips,
It was infectious.

It was hard to tell,
If it was her glittering eyes,
Or her pearl-white teeth,
That gleamed more.

When she laughed,
She squeezed her tiny eyes shut,
And forced them open,
Full to the brim, with happy tears.

Her hair was long,
Braided in two.
Her dreams were big,
Draped in leather.

When I saw her last,
Her eyes held the sparkle,
Of a thousand stars.
She lit up and made her own aura.

When I saw her last,
She smiled a smile,
Flashing her teeth,
Whiter than the sun.

When her poem reached me,
My heart was heavy.
For it carried the weight
Of our love and sisterhood.

The mark she set is indelible,
Unmatched, irreplaceable.
Like true love, such friends come once.
When they leave, you wait.

This one was short,
Maybe next would be longer.
I promise you the wait,
And you promise me time.

(34) The Grand Love

The grandest love,
That love has ever known,
Is several decades old.

The vastness and depths,
Of which,
No world can ever fathom.

The slight trembles
And heavy breaths,
Much like a lullaby.

Their rhythm felt home,
The warmth of hugs,
And the scent of herbs.

Their home was mine,
They were more mine.
The grandeur of love.

Enveloping me with their love,
They sung in unison,
Songs that were always off the beat.

They chased me around
With wobbly knees,
Strained breaths, yet cheerful laughter.

Grandiosity of this grand love,
Of them wanting to slow down,
Time, myself and themselves.

Of living a second chance,
At parenting, loving and holding
A whole new dream that is me.

(35) The Telly

The telly was always turned on,
Conversation less important,
Our eyes glued to it,
Looking at each other briefly.

The telly belonged to everyone,
Shows took their turns,
Sometimes an excuse,
To avoid serious talks.

Sometimes telly helped
Cover the awkward silences,
Evade the important,
Leave the food cold.

More often than not,
The chatter of telly
Was content,
It meant home was not far.

Years later,
Telly was just a background,
Its voice drowned
In the chatter and laughter.

Turned on still,
It was the sound of home,
Of a sweet past,
That anchored us in the same space.

36 Rotund

My grandfather was known,
For his big, round tummy.
He used to lift me
And place me right on it.

I used to pat on his belly,
His slow breaths had me
Rise and fall gently,
Like a little see-saw.

As I outgrew his belly,
He let me in his heart,
His betel nut coated teeth,
Only complementing his laugh.

We sat next to each other,
In my conflicts and calm,
In my silence and clamor,
In my depths and shallows.

His big belly comforted me,
In ways I did not know back then.
I came out of my mother's,
And landed right on his.

I stayed on his for longer,
My memories of his are vivid,
His love and warmth humongous,
Unbelievably unconditional.

Like King Mahabali,
Or Santa Claus,
Generous and big bellies,
My grandfather is my magic.

The hope in my despair,
Willingly pulling a chair next to me,
Reminding me to be him,
For those like me.

37 Love that Died

If I were to die,
Tell him,
That this life of mine,
Was half-lived.

That I lived, mostly,
In my head.
And outside my head,
I was by myself too.

That my life,
When it began,
I wanted to make it mine.
Completely.

That I wanted to own it,
And make it worthwhile.
All the back page scribbles
Were birthed and left behind.

That I was a passionate one,
Who never got tired,
Of the paradox called love,
Or the mysticism it carried.

That my love, was always
Powerful and bright,
It broke barriers and lit up
Everything, until it burned.

That my love sounded
Like the cracking of wood,
By the warmth you sought
On cold winter nights.

That no light could seep through
My blind eyes,
Which saw just him,
And a love I created around him.

That every time I cut myself,
I sucked my blood that tasted like him.
That every time I burned my hand,
It felt like nothing.

That nothing I did for him
Was ever enough for myself.
That his time meant the world to me.
That it scared me if I was not good enough.

That I wish I could tell him this
When I was still breathing,
But only if he looked at me,
Only if he remembered he had me.

(38) Cycle

Every month I bled,
It felt like I lost,
Parts of me I needed too.

The clots on the pad,
Looked like a piece of my insides-
A piece of my kidney?

Sometimes half of my intestine,
Or the rudimentary appendix,
The cramps solidified my fears.

Was period pain devised,
To safeguard procreation?
A nine-month hiatus to bribe women?

To sustain the species,
And to threaten women,
With months of blood-y torment?

Who does my womb
Get ready to house?
Who's coming in with no action?

My body, who keeps a watch
Of hundreds of viruses,
And has just the same antibodies.

Cannot keep track of action months,
To save me the other months,
From the futile bleeding.

It amuses me that,
Every period after baby,
Is a mere afterthought.

Instead of slowly churning out
My whole uterus and my inside every month,
Can I be pregnant with food forever?

39 Love Across Times

One of my births,
I was your pen.
I weighed just as much
As your thoughts did.

And all I birthed
Was bits of them.
Words—broken, chipped,
Words—whole, bursting with life.

In another, I was a flower,
The one you watered,
Nurtured, tended to,
And plucked off for someone.

In yet another,
I was your still-born.
Knowing only you,
A whole lifetime of just you.

40 · Hunger

If hunger were to begin
At one point in the body,
It'd be in my head.

Right next to love and longing,
Nestled between want
And the depths of despair.

If hunger were a person,
He'd leave me
When he feels I've had enough.

He'd fill me in ways
That would make sense,
That would fulfill my senses.

Once hunger hits, I'm different,
It alters me in minutes
Creeping into my body.

Its grip getting tighter,
Like it's all in my head,
Which pounds from inside.

Hunger feeds on myself,
Slowly eroding pieces
From all over me.

Hunger makes me raw,
Reminds me I'm an animal,
Who can kill if he wills.

For survival is the goal,
The anthem and the way,
The urge to eat and not be eaten.

41 You

When it rained last night,
It was me.

Remember?
You did not find a shade,
Nor a raincoat.

You were to drench,
Bits of your hair first,
And then all at once.

Out of nowhere,
I was in your mind,
And you let me in.

All over your mind,
And your body,
There was no you and me, but us.

The goosebumps,
The warmth in the cold,
And the chills.

Remember?
How you felt so full?
Like you did when we hugged.

That rain, was me.
Somehow you knew.
And I knew that you knew.

You didn't run.
You stayed.
For an entire rainy season.

And when it was over,
We yearned for the next and how-
To rain and to soak.

42 SHe

Born a boy,
Her desire to be a *she*
Was quelled and killed,
As she revolted and resisted her *he*.

The *he* and the *she*,
The perfect balance as it is,
The imbalance was colossal,
The damage was deep.

As much as she thought
She was enough,
Her mind desired,
Validation, affection.

As much as she opened up,
She tucked away most of herself,
Constantly mistrusted,
Continually scared and shielded herself.

She wrote but never let one read,
She danced with doors closed,
She sang in hushed whispers,
She drew with faded pencil strokes.

She was always too afraid,
To be seen and read,
Always too guarded,
But yearned to be seen and heard.

In her paradox, she had found her home.
Pulling the wrong people in,
And pushing the right ones away.
Her man self-protected her *she self*.

So when he walked in,
He hurt himself against her thorny walls,
He reached out to her beads-
She thought, to crush her.

But all he wanted was to make them,
Into a necklace she could wear every day,
To concerts and dates with him,
Or even the evening walks together.

She recklessly hid the beads away,
Her pieces that could not be touched,
Left a few behind in a hurry,
She took them to her core.

He rushed to take them,
As a namesake or a memoir.
She ran faster,
Like a prey does from its predator.

She killed him with words,
That changed him forever.
As he left, in his clenched wrists,
Were a few beads she never saw.

43 Let Go

When it was time to go,
I was not so graceful.
I whined, cried and held on.

Evenings at the beach,
Always remind me of us,
Of you and me.

You were the setting sun,
And I, the sky.
We had a day.

Come evening, you were to set,
And like the sun does to the sky,
You spread a little to me.

Blushed me a little red,
Crimson, orange, yellow,
All that I was, was you.

Thousands swarmed in,
The entire world
Had their eyes on us.

Of the beauty that they saw,
Of the poem you were,
Of everything we were.

Yet you didn't stay,
Faded away,
Slowly, but surely.

Not a minute longer? asked the sky,
Not a minute longer, said the sun.
And the grip loosened.

Yet when I had to leave,
I could only leave like the waves,
Whining, roaring and rolling.

Muddy and murky,
Taking bits of the shore,
Back with me.

While the sky
Had no sign of the sun,
The waves...

They barged into the shore,
And claimed the shore,
Like it was hers.

As she returns, she is,
More than the plain, salty water she was,
Pieces of the brown shore, with her.

Taken to the depths of her ocean,
To the seabed,
To make a home for him.

And leave the door open,
For one day,
He will be back home.

44   **Killer**

His eyes were not red,
Neither did he wear anger.
He had a soft smile,
And kind eyes.

Though he walked into me,
It was because I asked him to!
I was not a lamp, he wasn't a lion,
Or so I thought.

He cut my hair first,
He likes it short, he said.
Also pulled my short tops down
To cover my butts.

His grip was strong,
Words sharp, and gaze up.
As I grew smaller and smaller,
Shrunk to nothing slowly.

His kind eyes belied his true self,
Condescence masked with timidity.
Smirks concealed with hollow words,
I saw myself lose parts of myself.

The incomplete self I was,
Still loved fiercely.
But the killer had no resolve
To be kind, but only to kill.

So I died a slow death,
Tied my hands.
Refused to swim,
Left bubbles on the surface.

And the killer popped them,
The last signs of my being,
And punched the water,
For taking me too soon.

45 — Love I Need

If you love traveling with me,
Would you also love staying in with me?
Knowing what keeps me awake,
Where my mind wanders off to.

If you love the food I cook,
Think you would want to watch me?
Be with me in the kitchen,
As I talk about my amateur skills?

If you love to hug me tight,
Would you wanna know
My deepest fears and worries?
About how I feel when you let go soon?

If you think you can take my pain away,
Would you watch me struggle to forgive myself?
Would you be impatient as I learn to love myself?
Would you ask me why I am so deep in the pit?

When I break and bury my face in my hands,
Would you stay beside me?
Would you hold my hand,
Walk me through the rocks to the sand?

If you see me stare at you on the darkest nights,
Would you tug me closer and gently rock me to sleep?
Or would you look at me and go back to sleep?
Would you ask me what the bad dream was about?

If my thoughts are straight lines,
Would you be their tendrils?
If my mind is a spiral,
Would you be the anchor?

Do you think you can love me
Like you love a broken child?
Would you give up too soon?
Would you be around on the brightest days?

On days you doubt my progress,
Know that our love is a therapy,
Know that you're a diver,
Who has found me floating, head inside water.

46 The Reader

I took myself on a date,
To the library by the corner.
The first book I picked,
Smelled like an old dust jacket.

Yellow pages with black letters,
A story so old yet so fresh.
When I read it, the words
Crept into my brain.

Like dainty flowers,
They adorned my mind.
New spots touched,
With a wise charm.

Stories of an author,
Who was buried way too soon,
Stood before me
As my eyes ran over his book.

If souls had a resting place,
It's not a cemetery but a library.
Between books that have known
The heat of tears smeared on them.

A fossilized tiny bug,
Etched forever in it,
I moved to the next page,
Painfully aware of ephemeral bugs.

47 Home

I fell in love,
Slowly and hesitant,
And then all at once.

When I saw her,
She was laughing.
Happiness looked beautiful.

When I talked to her,
She had her hands tied,
Still offered what she could.

It felt like a prayer,
But not quite.
I walked past her.

On a bright day,
Was this kid at the park,
Gleaming and full of life.

Though weeks had passed,
Her face surfaced in my mind,
Like she had never left.

What if I set you free?
Would you talk like a prayer?
Would you still be a whisper?

Her eyes rolled around,
I waited for them to hold mine,
What if you leave again?

Oh! You have been with me since then!
Since then!
She held my hand, hers untied.

Falling in love with you,
I thought,
Would be a decision.

But now I know,
It was not.
I was only falling.

We never 'decide',
To fall.
Falls happen.

And then you pick yourself up,
Dust yourself,
Wipe your tears.

Touch where it hurts,
Look around,
And limp forward.

But with this fall,
I fell into a great depth,
It felt like water.

Maybe I was drowning,
I did get breathless,
And my body was floating.

But I never hit the rocks,
Neither did I swim,
I was alight in thin air.

I do not want to pick myself up,
Or dust myself,
I have happy tears.

If I were to touch where I am happy,
I would have to embrace myself.
I look around and see just us.

Dancing, laughing, sleeping,
Swaying to slow music,
Red wine in dim yellow lights.

A peck on the cheek,
Being lost in each other's eyes,
Holding hands, watching the sunset.

It is just us,
As I fall,
To greater depths.

Slow gravity,
Hard fall,
Happy us.

48 The News

You were so young,
Lived a short life.
I looked keenly at the picture,
On the front page of the newsprint.

The details were gore,
But I read it anyway.
My heart wrenched a little,
At the pain you lived and died to.

My face drooped,
Like a lifeless flower.
A similar case surfaced my mind,
Another short life of tragic end.

Her name was buried deep in my mind,
Couldn't recall it, nor her face.
My eyes landed on another news,
And this one got buried quickly too.

Perhaps to surface later,
When another no-one dies a gore death.
Something to feed on until,
They find the next bone to throw to me.

49 Grown Kids

Children-
With beards and gray hairs,
But children, nevertheless.

From awaiting playtime,
To awaiting weekends,
Time played its cruel ways.

Brought the children,
Closer to the reality,
That life is.

Slipping away like sand,
No matter how clenched,
Their fists were.

Slowly at first,
And then one day,
Loud cries became muffled screams.

From wounds that healed,
To cuts that always bled,
From pencils to pens.

Harder to erase and move on,
Childhood shrinks,
To a nostalgic emotion.

And adulthood roars,
Like a fierce but toothless lion,
Waiting to hit bed.

But children, nevertheless,
Taller by several feet,
But comfort is still home.

From jumping and giggling,
To limping and grimacing,
From being kids to having kids.

Time went by too fast,
Afterall, hands are so tiny,
To hold on to all things we love.

So we learn to let go more,
And hold on to less.
We think of the lost ones often.

And forget all that,
Our little hands hold,
While yearning for the lost.

50 Dreams

When I die,
Will someone take my dreams?
They're priceless,
Meant my whole life itself.

Because all my life,
I was living those dreams-
Inside my head,
Treading lightly not to drown.

If you'd take them,
Please water them every day,
Build a terrarium,
Just like I'm an ecosystem myself.

Bring the flowers they become
To my grave.
Bring the little bees along,
To sing for me.

And tell me quietly,
Like a prayer,
That when they wither away,
You'll bring new ones.

www.ingramcontent.com/pod-product-compliance
Lightning Source LLC
Chambersburg PA
CBHW062223150726
47991CB00006B/2411